BIG A

little   a

What begins with A?

3

Aunt Annie's alligator . . .

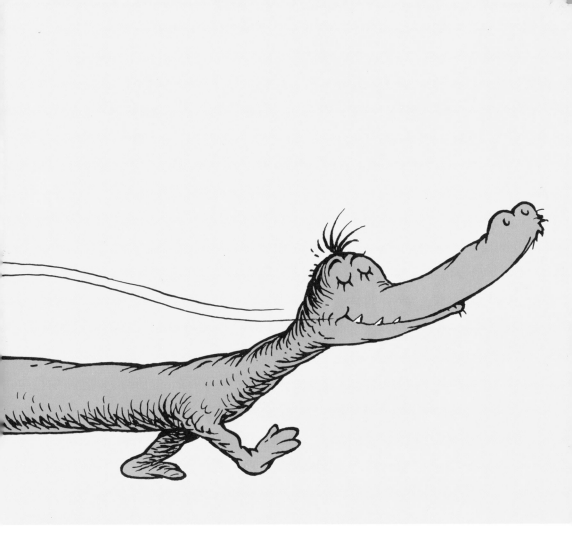

. . . . . . A . . a . . A

BIG B

little   b

What begins with B?

Barber
baby
bubbles
and a
bumblebee.

9

BIG C

little c

What begins with C?

Camel on the ceiling
C . . . . c C

BIG D

little d

David Donald Doo
dreamed
a dozen doughnuts
and
a duck-dog, too.

ABCDE..e..e

ear

egg

elephant

e

e

E

15

BIG F

little   f

F .. f .. F

Four fluffy feathers
on a
Fiffer-feffer-feff.

ABCD
EFG

Goat
girl
googoo goggles
G . . . g . . . G

BIG H

little   h

Hungry horse.
Hay.

Hen in a hat.
Hooray !
Hooray !

BIG I

little   i

i.... i.... i

Icabod
is
itchy.

So am I.

BIG J

little   j

What begins with j?

Jerry Jordan's
jelly jar
and jam
begin that way.

BIG K

little   k

Kitten. Kangaroo.

26

Kick a kettle.
Kite
and a
king's kerchoo.

BIG L
little   l

Little Lola Lopp.
Left leg.
Lazy lion
licks a lollipop.

BIG M

little   m

Many mumbling mice
are making
midnight music
in the moonlight . . .

mighty nice

BIG N

little n

What begins with those?

Nine new neckties
and a nightshirt
and a nose.

O is very useful.
You use it when you say:
"Oscar's only ostrich
oiled
an orange owl today."

ABCD
EFG
HIJK
LMNO...

...P

Painting pink pyjamas.
Policeman in a pail.

Peter Pepper's puppy.
And now
Papa's in the pail.

BIG Q

little   q

What begins with Q ?

The quick
Queen of Quincy
and her
quacking quacker-oo.

QUACK

QUACK

41

BIG R

little r

Rosy Robin Ross.

Rosy's going riding
on her
red rhinoceros.

BIG S

little   s

Silly Sammy Slick
sipped six sodas
and got
sick sick sick.

T . . . . . T

t . . . . t

What begins with T?

Ten tired turtles
on a tuttle-tuttle tree.

BIG U

little   u

What begins with U?

Uncle Ubb's umbrella
and his
underwear, too.

49

BIG V

little   v

Vera Violet Vinn
is
very
very
very awful
on her violin.

51

W...w...W

Willy Waterloo
washes Warren Wiggins
who is
washing Waldo Woo.

X is very useful
if your name is
Nixie Knox.
It also
comes in handy
spelling axe
and extra fox.

NIXIE KNOX

BIG Y

little   y

A yawning yellow yak.
Young Yolanda Yorgenson
is yelling on his back.

QRS
TUV...

W..X
Y.. and ....

BIG Z

little   z

What begins with Z?

I do.

I am a
Zizzer-Zazzer-Zuzz
as you can
plainly see.

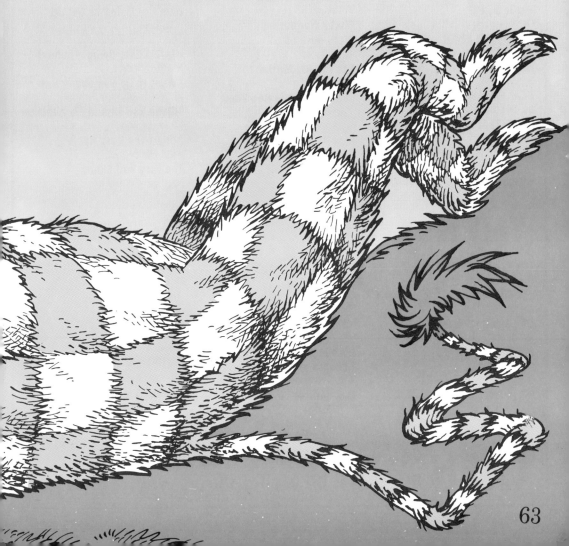

Learning to read is fun with Beginner Books

FIRST get started with:

Ten Apples Up On Top
Dr. Seuss

Go Dog Go
P D Eastman

Put Me in the Zoo
Robert LopShire

THEN gain confidence with:

Dr. Seuss's ABC*
Dr. Seuss

Fox in Sox*
Dr. Seuss

Green Eggs and Ham*
Dr. Seuss

Hop on Pop*
Dr. Seuss

I Can Read With My Eyes Shut
Dr. Seuss

I Wish That I Had Duck Feet
Dr. Seuss

One Fish, Two Fish*
Dr. Seuss

Oh, the Thinks You Can Think!
Dr. Seuss

Please Try to Remember the First of October
Dr. Seuss

Wacky Wednesday
Dr. Seuss

Are You My Mother?
P D Eastman

Because a Little Bug Went Ka-choo!
Rosetta Stone

Best Nest
P D Eastman

Come Over to My House
Theo. LeSieg

The Digging-est Dog
Al Perkins

I Am Not Going to Get Up Today!
Theo. LeSieg

It's Not Easy Being a Bunny!
Marilyn Sadler

I Want to Be Somebody New
Robert LopShire

Maybe You Should Fly a Jet!
Theo. LeSieg

Robert the Rose Horse
Joan Heilbroner

The Very Bad Bunny
Joan Heilbroner

THEN take off with:

The Cat in the Hat*
Dr. Seuss

The Cat in the Hat Comes Back*
Dr. Seuss

Oh Say Can You Say?
Dr. Seuss

My Book About Me
Dr. Seuss

A Big Ball of String
Marion Holland

Chitty Chitty Bang Bang!
Ian Fleming

A Fish Out of Water
Helen Palmer

A Fly Went By
Mike McClintock

The King, the Mice and the Cheese
N & E Gurney

Sam and the Firefly
P D Eastman

BERENSTAIN BEAR BOOKS
By Stan & Jan Berenstain

The Bear Detectives
The Bear Scouts
The Bears' Christmas
The Bears' Holiday
The Bears' Picnic
The Berenstain Bears and the Missing Dinosaur Bones
The Big Honey Hunt
The Bike Lesson

THEN you won't quite be ready to go to college. But you'll be well on your way!

*From the Dr. Seuss Classic Collection